THE DIDACHE

The Teaching of the Twelve Apostles,

Commonly Called

THE Didache

ISBN: 978-1-6673-0695-7 paperback
ISBN: 978-1-6673-0696-4 hardcover

INTRODUCTION

No document of the early church has proved so bewildering to scholars as this apparently innocent tract which was discovered by Philotheos Byrennios in 1873. The Didache or Teaching (for that is what the Greek word means) falls into two parts. The first is a code of Christian morals, presented as a choice between the way of life and the way of death. The second part is a manual of Church Order which, in a well-arranged manner, lays down some simple, at times even naïve, rules for the conduct of a rural congregation. It deals with such topics as baptism, fasting, the Lord's Supper, itinerant prophets, and the local ministry of bishops and deacons. It concludes with a warning paragraph on the approaching end of the world.

At one time this tract was viewed as a very ancient product—as early as A.D. 70 or 90. Recent study, however, has conclusively shown that, in the form we have it, it belongs to the second century. There is, nevertheless, no unanimity among scholars about its exact date or purpose. It has appropriately been called the "spoiled child of criticism"; and it will probably need a good deal more spoiling before its riddle is finally solved.

The "Two Ways"

The literary problem of the Didache is extremely complex and only the bare outlines can be sketched here. As it stands, the document bears a close relationship to several other early Christian writings. The moral catechism or "Two Ways" of its opening chapters (chs. 1 to 5) appears in a rather different version at the end of the Letter of Barnabas (between A.D. 100 and 130), and has also come down to us as an independent document in a Latin translation. Much of this material, furthermore, turns up in the fourth century Apostolic Church Order (with many interpolations) and in the *Life of Schnudi* (fifth century). The connection between all these documents has been very closely studied, and differing opinions are held about it. Some claim that the author of Barnabas invented the "Two Ways."[457] Others contend that the "Two Ways" was originally an independent catechism (perhaps Jewish in origin), and that it has been incorporated in different forms by the various compilers.[458] Perhaps the most reasonable explanation to account for the many complexities is as follows:

The "Two Ways" was an independent catechism current in several versions,[459] of which three have come down to us. None represents the original in its pure form. Barnabas' is the earliest version we possess, but it suffers from displacements, and here and there the author has freely rendered his source in his own style.[460] The second form is that found (with minor variations) in the Latin, the Apostolic Church Order, and the *Life of Schnudi.* This has preserved the original order, but it displays an ecclesiastical tendency[461] and has interpolated a further section (= Did. 3:1–6, commonly called "the fences"[462]). The final form is that in the Didache. It is distinguished by the addition of yet another insertion—sayings from the Gospels and other sources (chs. 1:3 to 2:1).

Date and Place of the Didache

The first five chapters of the Teaching, then, represent a late form of an original catechism into which the Didachist has inserted en bloc and not very neatly[463] some distinctively Christian sayings. They betray a knowledge of Matthew and Luke, and one is clearly derived from the Shepherd of Hermas (ch. 1:5 = Man. 2:4.–6), which was written about A.D. 100. Another indication of the date of the Didache is to be found in ch. 16, where a citation from the Letter of Barnabas appears (ch. 16:2 = Barn. 4:9). There can be little doubt that we are dealing with a second century document which reveals a wide canon of Scripture, including Barnabas and Hermas. The *terminus ad quem* is to be set by the quotations from the Teaching in a Syrian church order called the Didascalia. This dates from the early third century.

That the Didache comes from Alexandria[464] is suggested by several factors. The "Two Ways" was in circulation there, for the Letter of Barnabas and the Apostolic Church Order come from that locality. It is possible, but not certain, that Clement of Alexandria knew our Didache.[465] The Teaching's liberal attitude toward the New Testament canon, apparently including Barnabas and Hermas, bespeaks Alexandria. Furthermore, up to the fourth century the Teaching was highly regarded in Egypt, itself hovering on the verge of the canon, and being mentioned by Athanasius as suitable for catechetical reading (Festal Letter, ch. 39). Then again, Serapion of Thmuis (fourth century) has a quotation from the Didache in his Eucharistic prayer. In view of the conservative nature of these prayers, this is a weighty factor.

The Church Order of the Didache

The second part of the Teaching (chs. 6 to 15) is a manual of Church Order. It has generally been held that the Didachist himself wrote this section of the work, adding it to the "Two Ways." It poses, however, very difficult problems, and three main views are current about it. Some[466] claim that it faithfully reflects the subapostolic period in the rural churches of Syria. Others[467] hold that its regulations regarding prophets betray its Montanist origin. A third opinion[468] is that the Didache is an artificial composition, aimed to recall the second century Church to greater simplicity by reconstructing an imaginative picture of primitive Christianity from apostolic sources. This third view is most unlikely. Second century literature was never purely antiquarian in mode or interest. Its reconstructions of primitive times were directed toward giving apostolic warrant to newer ideas and customs. It is the absence from the Didache of such familiar themes as virginity, episcopacy, Gnostic and anti-Gnostic tendencies, which needs explaining.

The claim that the Didache is a Montanist tract has more to be said for it. Yet this view, too, is hardly tenable. The most characteristic Montanist features are lacking from the Teaching. It reflects nothing of Montanus and his prophetesses, of the ascetic rigor of that movement, of the high place accorded women, of the lively eschatology in connection with Pepuza, or of the opposition to second marriages and second repentance. On all these questions the Didache is silent. This disturbing fact has to be met by the further assumption that all clear traces of the New Prophecy were purposely suppressed in the interests of showing "how respectable and apostolic Montanism could be." This is, in short, an admission that the Teaching is not really Montanist.[469]

It is, then, to the first view that we are driven. While it is not without difficulties, it is less unlikely than the others. Some of these difficulties, moreover, can be removed if we do not follow the general assumption that the Didachist wrote this section of the tract himself. It is much more plausible to suppose that he was a compiler, rather than an author; and that, just as he made use of the "Two Ways" at the beginning, so in the second part of his work he utilized an early source for his Church Order. That would explain why his tract has such a curious appearance. Onto the catechism he has sewn some genuinely primitive regulations about Church life. The effect is very odd, for he implies that the moral catechism sufficed for baptismal instruction (ch. 7:1), which is, of course, contrary to all we know of early Christianity. Only a scribe with a limited number of sources at hand could have left such an impression. He did, indeed, try to rectify things a little by adding the gospel precepts. But that was the best he could do under the circumstances. It is not possible to tell how much of the Church Order he has faithfully preserved or how much he has altered. Yet his method of handling the "Two Ways" suggests that he would be more likely to make insertions en bloc than to change his source radically.

We should assume, then, that some scribe in Alexandria about A.D. 150 edited two ancient documents which came into his hands. One was the "Two Ways"; the other was a late first century set of regulations about Church life. He made some changes in them—how many we shall never know. He certainly added a section of sayings to the "Two Ways" and probably composed the final ch. 16, which is only loosely related to the rest of the document. It is noteworthy that an interest in perfection appears in these two places (chs. 1:4; 16:2) and in one other—at the junction of the two sources (ch. 6:2). It seems a mark of the Didachist. Moreover, it is only in his addition to the catechism and in ch. 16 that a wide knowledge of New Testament Scripture is evident. In these two places he conflates Matthew with Luke and cites, among other things, Barnabas and Hermas. The rest of the work reveals only a knowledge of Matthew's Gospel.

The Didache, thus, is the first of those fictitious Church Orders which edit ancient material and claim apostolic authorship. As in many such instances (e.g., the Apostolic Church Order, the Apostolic Constitutions, the Testament of Our Lord), we cannot be sure precisely what is original and what is edited. Nor do the various regulations necessarily apply to the time of the compilation. Sometimes a scribe will brush up ancient material sufficiently to make it appear relevant to his period. More often he will change it only a little, leaving a curious combination of the ancient and the modern, which is bewildering. Hence a degree of caution is needed in citing the Didache as a witness to first century customs. Yet the main outlines of its arrangements for Church life do seem to reflect the end of the first century before the monepiscopate had finally triumphed and while the gift of prophecy was still exercised (chs. 11; 13). Moreover, the Eucharistic prayers (chs. 9; 10),[470] so clearly modeled on the Jewish forms for grace before and after meals, betray a period when the Lord's Supper was still a real supper, and when the joyful and expectant note of the Messianic Banquet had not yet been obscured by the more solemn emphasis on the Lord's Passion.

To compile such a document must have been a congenial task for an Alexandrine scribe who adhered to the small Catholic minority in that city. Surrounded as he was by every novelty of Gnostic speculation, he would doubtless take a special delight in preserving the records of antiquity.

That the source of the Didache's Church Order (chs. 6:3 to 15) belongs to Syria and comes from the late first century may be gathered from several factors. It is clearly dependent upon Matthew's Gospel and so cannot be earlier than A.D. 90. This Gospel, it may be noted, probably comes from Syria. The Eucharistic prayers reflect an area where wheat is sown on the hillsides (ch. 9:4), and the baptismal section presupposes a vicinity where warm baths are prevalent (ch. 7:2). All these points bespeak Syria, though the Eucharistic prayers themselves may be Judean in origin. The prophets and teachers (chs. 11 and 13) forcibly recall the situation in Antioch where, according to Acts 13:1, the Church leaders were so named. We may remind ourselves that the author of The Acts is always careful about his titles.[471] The picture we gain from this source of the Didache is one of rural communities[472] periodically enjoying a visitation from the leaders of some Christian center. Indeed, a city like Antioch may well have been responsible for this primitive manual to guide the rural churches.

---

[457]So J. Armitage Robinson, J. Muilenburg, R. H. Connolly, F. C. Burkitt. See the section on Manuscripts and Books.

[458]So C. Taylor, A. Harnack (his later view), K. Kohler, B. H. Streeter, and J. M. Creed. E. Goodspeed holds that the Latin represents something like the original form.

[459]Jerome (De Vir. Ill. I) and Rufinus (In Symb. Apost., ch. 21) seem to have known it in some connection with Peter's name.

[460]That the version in Barnabas is secondary is clear from ch. 19:7, where he has displaced an injunction to slaves, referring it to all his readers. Furthermore, phrases that are most characteristic of Barnabas are absent from the other versions. This would hardly have happened if they all depended on him.

[461]Cf. Did. 4:1, 2; ch. 14 with Barn. 19:9, 10, 12.

[462]From the Jewish "fences" of the law.

[463]Note how the second command of the Teaching (2: 1) has been preceded by no first command. In an Oxyrhynchus fragment of the Didache a scribe has tried to iron this out by inserting in ch. 1:3, fin.: "Hear what you must do to save your spirit. First of all . . ."

[464]The Egyptian origin of the Didache was held by Byrennios, Zahn, and Harnack.

[465]See F. R. M. Hitchcock's article in The Journal of Theological Studies, 1923, pp. 397 ff.

[466]So B. H. Streeter, J. M. Creed, T. Klauser, and J. A. Kleist.

[467]So R. H. Connolly and F. E. Vokes. The suggestion goes back to Hilgenfeld.

[468]So J. Armitage Robinson. See also W. Telfer's "Antioch Hypothesis" in The Journal of Theological Studies, 1939, revised to a "Jerusalem Hypothesis," ibid., 1944.

[469]A Montanist, moreover, would never have put the prophetic ministry on a par with that of the local clergy; see ch. 15:1.

[470]Some (e.g., R. H. Connolly; also G. Dix, Shape of the Liturgy, pp. 90 ff., London, 1944) have held that these prayers refer not to the Eucharist proper, but to the "agapē," or Church supper. The difficul-

ties with this view are as follows: the supper is called "Eucharist," a term generally reserved for the Sacrament (cf. ch. 14:1); it is carefully guarded from profanation (ch. 9:5); and it follows the section on Baptism. What we anticipate is a treatment of the baptismal Eucharist such as we find in this place in other Church Orders. A description of the less significant "agapē" would interrupt the natural sequence in the writer's mind.

[471]That "prophets" was a title for leaders of the Church, next to the apostles, is indicated in I Cor. 12:28 and clear from Eph. 4:11. It is noteworthy that Matthew has two unique sayings about false prophets (chs. 7:15; 24:11; cf. 10:41). That Gospel evidently reflects the same problem faced by this source of the Didache (cf. ch. 11).

[472]Note the "first fruits" of ch. 13.

MANUSCRIPTS AND BOOKS

Manuscripts

Only one Greek text of the Didache has survived. It is the Jerusalem Codex discovered by Byrennios in 1873, and published by him in Constantinople ten years later. It was written by a scribe, Leo, in 1056. A photographic facsimile was published by J. Rendel Harris in 1887.

Two papyrus fragments of the Didache in Greek (chs. 1:3, 4 and 2:7 to 3:2) were edited by A. S. Hunt in *Oxyrhynchus Papyri,* 15, London, 1922, pp. 12–15.

The Greek texts of the Epistle of Barnabas (chs. 18 to 20) and of the Apostolic Church Order (chs. 1 to 13) contain the "Two Ways" material in different forms. In the latter case there are many additions, and dependence on the "Two Ways" breaks off at the equivalent of Did. 4:8. The Greek text of the Apostolic Constitutions (ch. 7:1–32) contains almost the whole of the Didache with a number of changes and many insertions.

In Syriac there are citations from the Didache in the Didascalia, edited by R. H. Connolly, Oxford University Press, London, 1929.

In Latin there is a third century translation of the "Two Ways." A fragment was published by B. Pez in 1723. The complete text was edited from an eleventh century manuscript by J. Schlecht, *Doctrina XII Apostolorum,* Freiburg, 1900.

In Coptic there is a fifth century papyrus fragment of chs. 10:3b to 12:2a, edited by G. Horner in *The Journal of Theological Studies,* 25, 1924, pp. 225–231. (It is notable for adding after the Eucharistic prayer a thanksgiving for myron, holy oil for confirmation.)

In Arabic the "Two Ways" material is found in the fifth century *Life of Schnudi.* A German rendering is given by L. E. Iselin and A. Heusler in Texte und Untersuchungen, XIII, 1b, pp. 6–10, 1895.

In Ethiopic the following parts of the Didache have been preserved in the Ecclesiastical Canons: chs. II:3–5, 7–11, 12; 12:1–5; 13:1, 3–7; 8:1, 2a, in that order. They are edited by G. Horner, *Statutes of the Apostles,* pp. 193, 194, London, 1904.

In Georgian there is a complete translation made in the fifth century by a scribe, Jeremias of Orhai. The variant readings were published by G. Peradze in *Zeitschrift für die neutestamentliche Wissenschaft,* pp. 111–116, 1932, from a copy of an eleventh century manuscript in Constantinople.

Books and Articles

The best Greek text, making use of all the available witnesses, is by Theodorus Klauser, *Doctrina Duodecim Apostolorum: Barnabae Epistula,* "Florilegium Patristicum," I, Bonn, 1940. It has been used for this translation. Also of importance are the texts in K. Bihlmeyer, *Die apostolischen Väter,* Tübingen, 1924 (note his treatment of the Coptic evidence pp. xviii–xx), in K. Lake, *The Apostolic Fathers,* London, 1912, and in H. Hemmer, G. Oger, and A. Lamont, *Les Pères apostoliques,* Vol. I, Paris, 1907 (based on the text of F. X. Funk, *Patres apostolici,* Tübingen, 1901).

Older editions of the Didache, which contain a number of the related documents along with the text of Byrennios, are by

A. Harnack, *Die Lehre der Zwölf Apostel,* Texte und Untersuchungen, II, Leipzig, 1884 (a pioneer and monumental work which includes the Greek text of the A. C. O. and the relevant parts of A. C. 7); and by Philip Schaff, *The Oldest Church Manual Called the Teaching of the Twelve Apostles,* New York, 1885 (includes the pertinent sections from Barnabas, Hermas, A. C. O., and A. C. 7).

In addition to the works of Schaff and Lake mentioned above, the following translations in English may be noted: C. Bigg, *The Doctrine of the Twelve Apostles* (revised by A. J. Maclean), London, 1922; F. X. Glimm, *The Apostolic Fathers,* in the series The Fathers of the Church, Cima Publishing Company, New York, 1947; J. A. Kleist, *The Didache, The Epistle of Barnabas,* etc., in the series Ancient Christian Writers, Newman Press, Westminster, Maryland, 1948; and E. Goodspeed, *The Apostolic Fathers: An American Translation,* New York, 1950.

In German there are renderings by F. Zeller, *Die apostolischen Väter,* Munich, 1918, in the 2d series of the Bibliothek der Kirchenväter; by R. Knopf, *Die Lehre der Zwölf Apostel: Die zwei Clemensbriefe,* Tübingen, 1920, in Handbuch zum N. T.; and by E. Hennecke, *Neutestamentliche Apocryphen,* 2d edition, Tübingen, 1924.

In French there is the translation by Hemmer, Oger, and Lamont already mentioned.

In Italian there are renderings by M. dal Pra, *La Didache,* Venice, 1938; and by G. Bosio, *I Padri apostolici,* Part I, Turin, 1940, in the series Corona Patrum Salesiana.

All these editions have introductions and notes. The most significant are by Harnack, Schaff, Hemmer, Bigg, Kleist, and

Knopf. While Klauser's introduction and notes (in Latin) are most concise, they are no less important.

Studies in the Didache are extremely numerous. Of special importance are the following books: C. Taylor, *The Teaching of the Twelve Apostles with Illustrations from the Talmud,* Cambridge, 1886; J. A. Robinson, *Barnabas, Hermas, and the Didache,* London, 1920 (a revision of chs. 1 and 3 was published posthumously with a preface by R. H. Connolly in *The Journal of Theological Studies,* 1934, pp. 113–146, 225–248); J. Muilenburg, *The Literary Relations of the Epistle of Barnabas and the Teaching of the Twelve Apostles,* Ph.D. thesis, Marburg, 1929; F. E. Vokes, *The Riddle of the Didache,* S.P.C.K., London, 1938.

For many years debate about the Didache has been carried on in *The Journal of Theological Studies.* The following articles are noteworthy: J. V. Bartlet, "The Didache Reconsidered," 1921, pp. 239–249; R. H. Connolly, "The Use of the Didache in the Didascalia," 1923, pp. 147–157; F. R. M. Hitchcock, "Did Clement of Alexandria Know the Didache?" *ibid.,* pp. 397–401; R. H. Connolly, "New Fragments of the Didache," 1924, pp. 151–153; F. C. Burkitt, "Barnabas and the Didache," 1932, pp. 25–27; R. H. Connolly, "The Didache in Relation to the Epistle of Barnabas," *ibid.,* pp. 237–253; C. T. Dix, "Didache and Diatessaron," 1933, pp. 242–250, with Connolly's reply, *ibid.,* pp. 346, 347; A. L. Williams, "The Date of the Epistle of Barnabas," *ibid.,* pp. 337–346; R. D. Middleton, "The Eucharistic Prayers of the Didache," 1935, pp. 259–267; H. G. Gibbins, "The Problem of the Liturgical Section of the Didache," *ibid.,* pp. 373–386; B. H. Streeter, "The Much-belaboured Didache," 1936, pp. 369–374; R. H. Connolly, "Barnabas and the Didache," 1937, pp. 165–167; and "Canon Streeter on the Didache," *ibid.,* pp.

364–379; J. M. Creed, "The Didache," 1938, 370–387; W. Telfer, "The Didache and the Apostolic Synod of Antioch," 1939, pp. 133–146, 258–271; J. E. L. Oulton, "Clement of Alexandria and the Didache," 1940, pp. 177–179; W. Telfer, "The 'Plot' of the Didache," 1944, pp. 141–151.

To these studies should be added K. Kohler's article "Didache" in the *Jewish Encyclopedia,* Vol. IV, 1903, pp. 585–588; Louis Finkelstein, "The Birkat Ha-Mazon," in *Jewish Quarterly Review,* 1928, pp. 211–262; C. H. Turner, "The Early Christian Ministry and the Didache" in his *Studies in Early Church History,* Oxford, 1912, pp. 1–32; B. H. Streeter's summary of his view in *The Primitive Church* (Appendix C), New York, 1929; R. H. Connolly, "The Didache and Montanism," and "Agape and Eucharist in the Didache," both in the *Downside Review,* 1937, pp. 339–347, 477–489; the treatment by H. Lietzmann in *The Beginnings of the Christian Church,* New York, 1937, pp. 270–274; and the important study by E. Goodspeed, "The Didache, Barnabas, and the Doctrina," in the *Anglican Theological Review,* 1945, pp. 228–247, reprinted in his *Apostolic Fathers: An American Translation,* New York, 1950, pp. 285–310.

Of German and French studies we may mention A. Harnack, *Die Apostellehre und die jüdischen zwei Wege,* Leipzig, 1886, 2d edition, 1896 (an expanded reprint of his article „Apostellehre" in *Realencyclopädie für protestantische Theologie und Kirche);* F. X. Funk, „Die Didache, Zeit und Verh ltnis zu den verwandten Schriften," and „Zur Didache, der Frage nach der Grundschrift und ihren Rezensionen," in *Kirchengeschichtliche Abhandlungen und Untersuchungen,* 2, Paderborn, 1907, pp. 108–141, 218–229; L. Wohleb, *Die lateinische Übersetzung der Didache kritisch und sprachlich untersucht,* Paderborn, 1913; M.

Dibelius, „Die Mahlgebete der Didache," in *Zeitschrift für die neutestamentliche Wissenschaft*, 1938, pp. 32–41; and H. Leclercq, „Didache," in *Dictionnaire d'archéologie chrétienne et de liturgie*, Vol. IV. I, Paris, 1920, cols. 772–798. For further notices of the literature see Leclercq; also A. Harnack, *Geschichte der altchristlichen Literatur*, Leipzig, 1893, Vol. I, pp. 86–92; O. Bardenhewer, *Geschichte der altkirchlichen Literatur*, Freiburg, 1913, Vol. I, pp. 90–103; B. Altaner, *Patrologie*, 2d edition, Freiburg, 1950, pp. 39, 40; and J. Quasten, *Patrology*, Vol. I, pp. 38, 39, Utrecht, 1950.

THE TEACHING OF THE TWELVE APOSTLES, COMMONLY CALLED THE DIDACHE

THE TEXT

The Lord's Teaching to the Heathen by the Twelve Apostles:

1 There are two ways, one of life and one of death; and between the two ways there is a great difference.

[2]Now, this is the way of life: "First, you must love God who made you, and second, your neighbor as yourself."[473] And whatever you want people to refrain from doing to you, you must not do to them.[474]

[3]What these maxims teach is this: "Bless those who curse you," and "pray for your enemies." Moreover, fast "for those who persecute you." For "what credit is it to you if you love those who love you? Is that not the way the heathen act?" But "you must love those who hate you,"[475] and then you will make no enemies. [4]"Abstain from carnal passions."[476] If someone strikes you "on the right cheek, turn to him the other too, and you will be perfect."[477] If someone "forces you to go one mile with him, go along with him for two"; if someone robs you "of your overcoat, give him your suit as well."[478] If someone deprives you of "your property, do not ask for it back."[479] (You could not get it back anyway!) [5]"Give to everybody who begs from you, and ask for no return."[480] For the Father wants his own gifts to be universally shared. Happy is the man who gives as the commandment bids him, for he is guiltless! But alas for the man who receives! If he receives because he is in

need, he will be guiltless. But if he is not in need he will have to stand trial why he received and for what purpose. He will be thrown into prison and have his action investigated; and "he will not get out until he has paid back the last cent."[481] [6] Indeed, there is a further saying that relates to this: "Let your donation sweat in your hands until you know to whom to give it."[482]

2 The second commandment of the Teaching: [2] "Do not murder; do not commit adultery"; do not corrupt boys; do not fornicate; "do not steal"; do not practice magic; do not go in for sorcery; do not murder a child by abortion or kill a new-born infant. "Do not covet your neighbor's property; [3]do not commit perjury; do not bear false witness";[483] do not slander; do not bear grudges. [4]Do not be double-minded or double-tongued, for a double tongue is "a deadly snare."[484] [5] Your words shall not be dishonest or hollow, but substantiated by action. [6] Do not be greedy or extortionate or hypocritical or malicious or arrogant. Do not plot against your neighbor. [7] Do not hate anybody; but reprove some, pray for others, and still others love more than your own life.

3 My child, flee from all wickedness and from everything of that sort. [2]Do not be irritable, for anger leads to murder. Do not be jealous or contentious or impetuous, for all this breeds murder.

[3]My child, do not be lustful, for lust leads to fornication. Do not use foul language or leer, for all this breeds adultery.

[4]My child, do not be a diviner, for that leads to idolatry. Do not be an enchanter or an astrologer or a magician. More-

over, have no wish to observe or heed such practices, for all this breeds idolatry.

[5]My child, do not be a liar, for lying leads to theft. Do not be avaricious or vain, for all this breeds thievery.

[6]My child, do not be a grumbler, for grumbling leads to blasphemy. Do not be stubborn or evil-minded, for all this breeds blasphemy.

[7]But be humble since "the humble will inherit the earth."[485] [8] Be patient, merciful, harmless, quiet, and good; and always "have respect for the teaching"[486] you have been given. Do not put on airs or give yourself up to presumptuousness. Do not associate with the high and mighty; but be with the upright and humble. Accept whatever happens to you as good, in the realization that nothing occurs apart from God.

4 My child, day and night "you should remember him who preaches God's word to you,"[487] and honor him as you would the Lord. For where the Lord's nature is discussed, there the Lord is. [2] Every day you should seek the company of saints to enjoy their refreshing conversation. [3]You must not start a schism, but reconcile those at strife. "Your judgments must be fair."[488] You must not play favorites when reproving transgressions. [4]You must not be of two minds about your decision.[489]

[5] Do not be one who holds his hand out to take, but shuts it when it comes to giving. [6] If your labor has brought you earnings, pay a ransom for your sins. [7] Do not hesitate to give and do not give with a bad grace; for you will discover who He is that pays you back a reward with a good grace. [8]Do not turn your back on the needy, but share everything with your brother and call nothing your own. For if you have what is

eternal in common, how much more should you have what is transient!

[9]Do not neglect your responsibility[490] to your son or your daughter, but from their youth you shall teach them to revere God. [10] Do not be harsh in giving orders to your slaves and slave girls. They hope in the same God as you, and the result may be that they cease to revere the God over you both. For when he comes to call us, he will not respect our station, but will call those whom the Spirit has made ready. [11]You slaves, for your part, must obey your masters with reverence and fear, as if they represented God.

[12] You must hate all hypocrisy and everything which fails to please the Lord. [13]You must not forsake "the Lord's commandments," but "observe" the ones you have been given, "neither adding nor subtracting anything."[491] [14]At the church meeting you must confess your sins, and not approach prayer with a bad conscience. That is the way of life.

5 But the way of death is this: First of all, it is wicked and thoroughly blasphemous: murders, adulteries, lusts, fornications, thefts, idolatries, magic arts, sorceries, robberies, false witness, hypocrisies, duplicity, deceit, arrogance, malice, stubbornness, greediness, filthy talk, jealousy, audacity, haughtiness, boastfulness.[492]

[2]Those who persecute good people, who hate truth, who love lies, who are ignorant of the reward of uprightness, who do not "abide by goodness"[493] or justice, and are on the alert not for goodness but for evil: gentleness and patience are remote from them. "They love vanity,"[494] "look for profit,"[495] have no pity for the poor, do not exert themselves for the oppressed, ignore their Maker, "murder children,"[496]

corrupt God's image, turn their backs on the needy, oppress the afflicted, defend the rich, unjustly condemn the poor, and are thoroughly wicked. My children, may you be saved from all this!

6 See "that no one leads you astray"[497] from this way of the teaching, since such a one's teaching is godless.

[2]If you can bear the Lord's full yoke, you will be perfect. But if you cannot, then do what you can.

[3]Now about food: undertake what you can. But keep strictly away from what is offered to idols, for that implies worshiping dead gods.

7 Now about baptism: this is how to baptize. Give public instruction on all these points, and then "baptize" in running water, "in the name of the Father and of the Son and of the Holy Spirit."[498] [2] If you do not have running water, baptize in some other. [3]If you cannot in cold, then in warm. If you have neither, then pour water on the head three times "in the name of the Father, Son, and Holy Spirit."[499] [4]Before the baptism, moreover, the one who baptizes and the one being baptized must fast, and any others who can. And you must tell the one being baptized to fast for one or two days beforehand.

8 Your fasts must not be identical with those of the hypocrites.[500] They fast on Mondays and Thursdays; but you should fast on Wednesdays and Fridays.

[2]You must not pray like the hypocrites,[501] but "pray as follows"[502] as the Lord bid us in his gospel:

"Our Father in heaven, hallowed be your name; your Kingdom come; your will be done on earth as it is in heaven; give us today our bread for the morrow; and forgive us our debts as we forgive our debtors. And do not lead us into temptation, but save us from the evil one, for yours is the power and the glory forever."

3You should pray in this way three times a day.

9 Now about the Eucharist:[503] This is how to give thanks: 2First in connection with the cup:[504]

"We thank you, our Father, for the holy vine[505] of David, your child, which you have revealed through Jesus, your child. To you be glory forever."

3Then in connection with the piece[506] [broken off the loaf]:

"We thank you, our Father, for the life and knowledge which you have revealed through Jesus, your child. To you be glory forever.

4"As this piece [of bread] was scattered over the hills[507] and then was brought together and made one, so let your Church be brought together from the ends of the earth into your Kingdom. For yours is the glory and the power through Jesus Christ forever."

5You must not let anyone eat or drink of your Eucharist except those baptized in the Lord's name. For in reference to this the Lord said, "Do not give what is sacred to dogs."[508]

10 After you have finished your meal, say grace[509] in this way:

[2]"We thank you, holy Father, for your sacred name which you have lodged[510] in our hearts, and for the knowledge and faith and immortality which you have revealed through Jesus, your child. To you be glory forever.

[3]"Almighty Master, 'you have created everything'[511] for the sake of your name, and have given men food and drink to enjoy that they may thank you. But to us you have given spiritual food and drink and eternal life through Jesus, your child.

[4]"Above all, we thank you that you are mighty. To you be glory forever.

[5]"Remember, Lord, your Church, to save it from all evil and to make it perfect by your love. Make it holy, 'and gather' it 'together from the four winds'[512] into your Kingdom which you have made ready for it. For yours is the power and the glory forever."

[6]"Let Grace[513] come and let this world pass away."

"Hosanna to the God of David!"[514]

"If anyone is holy, let him come. If not, let him repent."[515]

"Our Lord, come!"[516]

"Amen."[517]

[7]In the case of prophets, however, you should let them give thanks in their own way.[518]

11 Now, you should welcome anyone who comes your way and teaches you all we have been saying. [2] But if the teacher proves himself a renegade and by teaching otherwise contradicts all this, pay no attention to him. But if his teaching furthers the Lord's righteousness and knowledge, welcome him as the Lord.

3Now about the apostles and prophets: Act in line with the gospel precept.[519] 4 Welcome every apostle on arriving, as if he were the Lord. 5 But he must not stay beyond one day. In case of necessity, however, the next day too. If he stays three days, he is a false prophet. 6On departing, an apostle must not accept anything save sufficient food to carry him till his next lodging. If he asks for money, he is a false prophet.

7While a prophet is making ecstatic utterances,[520] you must not test or examine him. For "every sin will be forgiven," but this sin "will not be forgiven."[521] 8However, not everybody making ecstatic utterances is a prophet, but only if he behaves like the Lord. It is by their conduct that the false prophet and the [true] prophet can be distinguished. 9For instance, if a prophet marks out a table in the Spirit,[522] he must not eat from it. If he does, he is a false prophet. 10 Again, every prophet who teaches the truth but fails to practice what he preaches is a false prophet. 11But every attested and genuine prophet who acts with a view to symbolizing the mystery of the Church,[523] and does not teach you to do all he does, must not be judged by you. His judgment rests with God. For the ancient prophets too acted in this way. 12But if someone says in the Spirit, "Give me money, or something else," you must not heed him. However, if he tells you to give for others in need, no one must condemn him.

12 Everyone "who comes" to you "in the name of the Lord"[524] must be welcomed. Afterward, when you have tested him, you will find out about him, for you have insight into right and wrong. 2 If it is a traveler who arrives, help him all you can. But he must not stay with you more than two days, or, if necessary, three. 3 If he wants to settle with you and is an artisan, he must work for his living. [4] If, however, he has no trade, use your judgment in taking steps for him to live with you as a Christian without being idle.[5] If he refuses to do this, he is trading on Christ. You must be on your guard against such people.

13 Every genuine prophet who wants to settle with you "has a right to his support." [2]Similarly, a genuine teacher himself, just like a "workman, has a right to his support."[525] [3] Hence take all the first fruits of vintage and harvest, and of cattle and sheep, and give these first fruits to the prophets. For they are your high priests. [4]If, however, you have no prophet, give them to the poor. [5]If you make bread, take the first fruits and give in accordance with the precept.[526] [6] Similarly, when you open a jar of wine or oil, take the first fruits and give them to the prophets. [7]Indeed, of money, clothes, and of all your possessions, take such first fruits as you think right, and give in accordance with the precept.

14 On every Lord's Day—his special day[527] —come together and break bread and give thanks, first confessing your sins so that your sacrifice may be pure. [2] Anyone at variance with his neighbor must not join you, until they are reconciled, lest your sacrifice be defiled. [3]For it was of this sacrifice that the Lord said, "Always and everywhere offer me a pure sacrifice; for I am a great King, says the Lord, and my name is marveled at by the nations."[528]

15 You must, then, elect for yourselves bishops and deacons who are a credit to the Lord, men who are gentle, generous, faithful, and well tried. For their ministry to you is identical with that of the prophets and teachers. [2]You must not, therefore, despise them, for along with the prophets and teachers they enjoy a place of honor among you.

[3] Furthermore, do not reprove each other angrily, but quietly, as you find it in the gospel. Moreover, if anyone has wronged his neighbor, nobody must speak to him, and he must not hear a word from you, until he repents. [4]Say your prayers, give your charity, and do everything just as you find it in the gospel of our Lord.

16 "Watch" over your life: do not let "your lamps" go out, and do not keep "your loins ungirded"; but "be ready," for "you do not know the hour when our Lord is coming."[529] [2]Meet together frequently in your search for what is good for your souls, since "a lifetime of faith will be of no advantage"[530] to you unless you prove perfect at the very last. [3] For in the final days multitudes of false prophets and seducers will appear. [4]Sheep will turn into wolves, and love into hatred. For with the increase of iniquity men will hate, persecute, and betray each other. And then the world deceiver will appear in the guise of God's Son. He will work "signs and wonders"[531] and the earth will fall into his hands and he will commit outrages such as have never occurred before. [5]Then mankind will come to the fiery trial "and many will fall away"[532] and perish, "but those who persevere" in their faith "will be saved"[533] by the Curse himself.[534] [6]Then "there will appear the signs"[535] of the Truth: first the sign of stretched-out [hands] in heaven,[536] then the sign of "a trumpet's blast,"[537] and thirdly the resurrection of the dead, though not of all the dead, [7]but as it has been said: "The Lord will come and all his saints with him. Then the world will see the Lord coming on the clouds of the sky."[538]

[473]Matt. 22:37–39; Lev. 19:18.

[474]Cf. Matt. 7:12.

[475]Matt. 5:44, 46, 47; Luke 6:27, 28, 32, 33.

[476]I Peter 2:11.

[477]Matt. 5:39, 48; Luke 6:29.

[478]Matt. 5:40, 41.

[479]Luke 6:30.

[480]Ibid.

[481]Matt. 5:26. This whole section 5 should be compared with Hermas, Mand. 2:4–7, on which it is apparently dependent.

[482]Source unknown.

[483]Ex. 20:13–17; cf. Matt. 19:18; 5:33.

[484]Prov. 21:6.

[485]Ps. 37:11; Matt. 5:5.

[486]Isa. 66:2.

[487]Heb. 13:7.

[488]Deut. 1:16, 17; Prov. 31:9.

[489]Meaning uncertain.

[490]Literally, "Do not withold your hand from . . ."

[491]Deut. 4:2; 12:32.

[492]Cf. Matt. 15:19; Mark 7:21, 22; Rom. 1:29–31; Gal. 5:19–21.

[493]Rom. 12:9.

[494]Ps. 4:2.

[495]Isa. 1:23.

[496]Wis. 12:6.

[497]Matt. 24:4.

[498]Matt. 28:19.

[499]Ibid.

[500]I.e., the Jews. Cf. Matt. 6:16.

[501]Matt. 6:5.

[502]Cf. Matt. 6:9–13.

[503]I.e., "the Thanksgiving." The term, however, had become a

technical one in Christianity for the special giving of thanks at the Lord's Supper. One might render the verbal form ("give thanks"), which immediately follows, as "say grace," for it was out of the Jewish forms for grace before and after meals (accompanied in the one instance by the breaking of bread and in the other by sharing a common cup of wine) that the Christian thanksgivings of the Lord's Supper developed.

[504]It is a curious feature of the Didache that the cup has been displaced from the end of the meal to the very beginning. Equally curious is the absence of any direct reference to the body and blood of Christ.

[505]This may be a metaphorical reference to the divine life and knowledge revealed through Jesus (cf. ch. 9:3). It may also refer to the Messianic promise (cf, Isa. 11:1), or to the Messianic community (cf. Ps. 80:8), i.e., the Church.

[506]An odd phrase, but one that refers to the Jewish custom (taken over in the Christian Lord's Supper) of grace before meals. The head of the house would distribute to each of the guests a piece of bread broken off a loaf, after uttering the appropriate thanksgiving to God.

[507]The reference is likely to the sowing of wheat on the hillsides of Judea.

[508]Matt. 7:6.

[509]Or "give thanks." See note 47.

[510]For the phrase cf. Neh. 1:9.

[511]Wis. 1:14; Sir. 18:1; Rev. 4:11.

[512]Matt. 24:31.

[513]A title for Christ.

[514]Cf. Matt. 21:9, 15.

[515]Or perhaps "be converted."

[516]Cf. I Cor. 16:22.

[517]These terse exclamations may be versicles and responses. More likely they derive from the Jewish custom of reading verses concerning Israel's future redemption and glory, after the final benediction.

[518]I.e., they are not bound by the texts given.

[519]Matt. 10:40, 41.

[520]Literally, "speaking in a spirit," i.e., speaking while possessed by a divine or demonic spirit. This whole passage (ch. 11:7–12) is a sort of parallel to Matt. 12:31 ff. There is an interpretation of the sin against the Holy Ghost, followed by a comment on good and evil conduct (cf. Matt. 12:33–37), and concluded by the prophets' signs which are suggested by the sign of the Son of Man (Matt. 22:38 ff.).

[521]Matt. 12:31.

[522]The sense is not clear, but suggests a dramatic portrayal of the Messianic banquet. It was characteristic of the Biblical prophets to drive home their teaching by dramatic and symbolic actions (cf. Jer., ch. 19; Acts 21:11; etc.) .

[523]Literally, "acts with a view to a worldly mystery of the Church." The meaning is not certain, but some dramatic action, symbolizing the mystical marriage of the Church to Christ, is probably intended. The reference may, indeed, be to the prophet's being accompanied by a spiritual sister (cf. I Cor 7:36 ff.).

[524]Matt. 21:9; Ps. 118:26; cf. John 5:43.

[525]Matt. 10:10. The provision for the prophet or teacher to settle and to be supported by the congregation implies the birth of the monarchical episcopate. Note the connection of this with the high priesthood (cf. Hippolytus, Apost. Trad. 3:4) and tithing. No provision is made for the support of the local clergy in ch. 15.

[526]Deut. 18:3–5.

[527]Literally, "On every Lord's Day of the Lord."

[528]Mal. 1:11, 14.

[529]Matt. 24:42, 44; Luke 12:35.

[530]Barn. 4:9.

[531]Matt. 24:24.

[532]Matt. 24:10.

[533]Matt. 10:22; 24:13.

[534]An obscure reference, but possibly meaning the Christ who suffered the death of one accursed (Gal. 3:13; Barn. 7:9). Cf. two other titles for the Christ: Grace (ch. 10:6) and Truth (v. 6).

[535]Matt. 24:30.

[536]Another obscure reference, possibly to the belief that the Christ would appear on a glorified cross. Cf Barn. 12:2–4.

[537]Matt. 24:31.

[538]Zech. 14:5; I Thess. 3:13; Matt. 24:30.

www.ingramcontent.com/pod-product-compliance
Lightning Source LLC
Chambersburg PA
CBHW071803020426
42331CB00008B/2383
* 9 7 8 1 6 6 7 3 0 6 9 5 7 *